PRAISE FOR D

At Zappos.com, our core values include pursuing growth and learning, doing more with less, and building a positive team and family spirit. Dave's message can resonate with anyone looking to live those values and make themselves invaluable.

—**Tony Hsieh**, CEO, Zappos.com

Dave Crenshaw demonstrates how multitasking is, in fact, a lie that actually wastes time, energy, and money... 'switchtasking', as Dave calls it, not only uses up more of our resources, but it also diminishes our overall productivity.

—**Chuck Norris**, Actor and Martial Artist

Crenshaw has mastered the perfect recipe for small business success. This book rocks!

—**Michael Symon**, Iron Chef and Restaurateur

We live in an ADHD world. And I'm glad we do. But as Dave understands, the secret is to do one important thing at a time, with focus. If you can take the time to focus on his message, you'll be glad you did.

—**Seth Godin**, Author, *Tribes*

As someone who has lived the tale Dave Crenshaw tells, focus always triumphs over chaos! Don't be attracted to all shiny objects; find the right object and make it shine!

—**Lynda Weinman**, Cofounder of Lynda.com

i

This is the one book I wished I had when I first started out in business. The Focused Business is jam-packed with street-smart strategies to help you achieve success NOW. Crenshaw rips apart all your excuses and will jump-start you on your way to the profits you deserve!

—**Dave Anderson**, Founder of "Famous Dave's"

Dave has perfectly captured the sobering reality of an entrepreneurial existence. Follow his advice and your path to excellence and the 'ultimate harvest' will be more rewarding and a lot less stressful. I wish this book existed five years ago.

—**Raegan Moya-Jones**, CEO and co-founder of Aden & Anais

Invaluable bridges the gap between employee – manager relationships and productivity. Companies that implement this message not only stand to improve their bottom line but also make their work environments happier for everyone.

—**Keith Ferrazzi**, Author, *Never Eat Alone*

Invaluable is the next logical step in career development. This story will show you step-by-step how to increase your value in the market and increase workplace harmony.

—**Daniel Pink**, Author, *A Whole New Mind* and *Drive*

This is a refreshingly honest and inventive approach to small business! I love it.

—**Neil Grimmer**, CEO and cofounder of Plum Organics

DAVE CRENSHAW

The Result

THE PRACTICAL, PROVEN FORMULA
FOR
GETTING WHAT YOU WANT

Crenshaw, Dave 1975-

The result : the practical, proven formula for getting what you want / Dave Crenshaw

ISBN-13: 978-0-9891936-4-1 (pbk.)
ISBN-13: 978-0-9891936-3-4 (e-book)

Printed in the United States of America.
Published by Invaluable Press
Herriman, Utah, USA

Cover design by Daniel Tesser
Interior formatting by John Arce

CONTENTS

For all my clients, past and present.

Your experiences and wisdom helped form this book. Thank you.

CHAPTER 1

The Question

What result do you want?

Simple question, is it not? Yet, it is perhaps the most powerful question to consider before completing any task, writing any document, or talking to any person. I'm not merely asking what it is that you *want*. I'm asking about what you want that you *don't* have at this moment.

In my twenty plus years of business and leadership coaching, I've found that asking my clients the question, "What result do you want, that you're not getting right now?" early in the process is critical to their success. It's critical to your success as well, even if you're flying solo.

So, take a moment and consider your answer to the question:

"WHAT RESULT DO I WANT THAT I'M NOT GETTING RIGHT NOW?"

My guess is, you didn't really consider the question. You didn't set the book aside and ponder your answer. You jumped to reading the next line. Am I right? If so, don't feel bad. You're certainly not alone.

The challenge with a question like this is that the world is a busy place. We're continually tempted to lose sight of the bigger picture. Once we're in the thick of things, we move fast...super fast. We jump from email to text to video conferencing to checking IMDB for the name of that actor we're thinking about to glancing at sports scores to responding to a quick question from a coworker to finding out what Fabio looks like right now— because the headline said it will make me gasp! And that was just in the last five minutes.

We multitask at dizzying speeds so much that we don't have the time to stop and ask ourselves the truly important questions. For all our busy-ness and get-it-done attitude, we can't see the forest for the tree we're about to walk headlong into, face down in a glowing screen.

I've found most people's aspirational horizon focuses on what they can accomplish within the next two weeks...at best. People increasingly tell me that they feel empty at work. While they've become more digitally connected to the world, they've grown disconnected from people and feelings. They're just doing stuff and going nowhere.

Being busy should not be the goal of one's career. Getting results should be.

Yet, when asked how we're doing, why do so many of us respond by defining ourselves by this *b-word*? And make no mistake: "busy" is about the dirtiest four-letter word you can utter. Being busy is not a sign of success; it is a white flag of surrender.

Time to take back control and create terms of unconditional, lasting victory.

RUBBING THE LAMP

One of my favorite movies growing up was Disney's *Aladdin*. Behind the talking parrot, musical numbers, and flying throw rug hides this "result" question I keep referring to. When Aladdin rubs the lamp and the genie pops out with joy in his heart and a Jack Nicholson impression in his back pocket, he's ready to give Aladdin the moon and stars.

Think of this book as that genie in a bottle. Go on, rub the lamp and wish for something! What'll it be, master?

What result do you want?

Now, unlike the genie, we're limited by the basic principles of physics and fundamental logic. For instance, I can't take you, all five feet and four inches of you, and—*voila!*—magically transform you into a star NBA center.

What this book *can* do, within the limits of the laws of the universe, is help you achieve your dreams. It is a reality. It can happen, and I've seen it happen repeatedly over two decades of working with people around the world.

The formula I'm going to show you to help you get the result you want is surprisingly rather simple. It isn't easy, though. You'll get out what you put into this book. If you work this simple system, you will achieve the result.

But first, you must decide what result you want. The genie can't make your wishes come true without a clearly defined outcome.

Let's suppose you're struggling to come up with an answer to that question at this moment. Don't sweat it. That's completely natural. In the coming chapters, we'll work together to help you get clear about what you want.

For now, consider three major areas.

THE CAREER RESULT

First, there's your **career**. This broad category covers everything from getting a new job to getting a raise, to moving to a better location, or to climbing the ladder of titles.

If improving your career is something you're interested in, it's possible you're missing a key component. So many people focus on the number of zeros on the paycheck that rolls in twice a month, which is all well and good. However, looking at your annual salary is skewing your perspective.

Suppose you're at a party and you meet two people. Person A tells you that they make $80,000 per year. Person B tells you that they also make $80,000 per year. You might start to think that they are doing about the same and fairly well for themselves. However, you then ask a couple follow-up questions. You find out that Person A works at least *seventy hours per week* to earn that $80,000, while Person B works *thirty hours per week* to make the same amount. Now, tell me: Which one is more successful?

Everyone's career aspirations may be a little different. Heck, maybe seventy hours per week is practically heaven for you. I'm not here to judge. However, focusing on increasing your value per hour can transform your career and give you the freedom to live the kind of life you've been dreaming of.

Whatever result you want for your career, define it, write it down, and focus on it.

THE PERSONAL RESULT
The second type of result that people look to get relates to their **personal** life. That might be something physical, like running a marathon or losing some weight. It may be something interpersonal, like improving your relationship with loved ones and spending more time with your children. It might mean something emotional or spiritual, like being a better listener or going out into the woods and letting the profound quiet heal your soul.

Occasionally, I'll get asked what my definition of success is. The truth is, my definition of success is personal to me—and yours should be too. Success is living the kind of life you want to live. Who am I to tell you what is right or wrong for you? I can't determine how many children you have, or what you have for dinner tonight, or where you should go on a Friday night. Like the genie said, *your* wish is my command.

So, whatever the kind of life you want looks like, get clear about it. Become intentional. Define the result you want in your life...that you're *not* getting right now.

THE ORGANIZATIONAL RESULT

Finally, think about the result you want for your organization. I'll use the term "organization" as it refers to any group of people working together for a common purpose, be it a for-profit business, nonprofit cause, school, branch of the FBI, or intramural ultimate frisbee team. All organizations are trying to get results. Businesses want to increase sales, managers want to increase customer satisfaction, teachers want to improve test scores. You get the picture!

If your organization is working to achieve a result, this book can help. That's really where this book began—in the catacombs of small organizations. I worked with business owners to grow their business and achieve more freedom within it. I practiced and honed the principles you learn here by working with entrepreneurs to help them get the results they wanted. As my audience diversified, I discovered that the principles taught here are universal and can be applied to any size of organization…or even just the individual.

Yet, all too often, organizations forget to keep growing—to continually pursue a greater result. Success is a dangerous thing, because it can make people complacent. As Jeff Bezos wisely said, "Day 2 is stasis. Followed by irrelevance. Followed by excruciating, painful decline. Followed by death. And that is why it is always Day 1." Continually asking, "What result do we want that we're not getting right now?" is, to me, the essence of keeping your organization in Day 1 and continually improving.

Of course, don't feel stifled by the three categories I've presented. I'm just trying to give you a map with commonly trod-upon trails. Don't be afraid to blaze your own.

Now, let's begin the process of answering this most important question:

WHAT RESULT DO YOU WANT?

CHAPTER 2:

The Result

Part of continual improvement is repeatedly pondering the question, "What result do I want that I'm not getting right now?" As you work to find an answer, you'll want to keep two principles in mind: focus and specificity.

Focus means trying to get one result at a time. A CEO I was working with once told me he wanted to simultaneously increase client retention and lower employee turnover. While these are both noble and worthy goals, they were too much to tackle at once. As we further discussed the most important issues, he realized that, at the moment, it was best to focus on client retention.

When some leaders talk about their key goals, I receive a diatribe that's half grocery list and half confession. Their results take a full two minutes to explain. You're not going to achieve the first result on your list if you're already thinking about the other nine.

There's a quote credited to Confucius that I love: "The man who chases two rabbits, catches neither." My book, *The Myth of Multitasking*, explores this concept at a micro level, yet it is equally true on the macro, strategic level. You must chase only one rabbit, because if you do not, you will not get *any* of the results. Focus on one result at a time.

Next is the principle of **specificity**. Specificity refers to clarity of intent. For example, saying that you're going to "lose some weight" doesn't really help you much. It's just not specific enough. Instead, your result should be exactly what you want to do and when you want to do it.

"I'm going to lose ten pounds within two months from today."

That's more like it!

THE RESULT HOUR

Gaining focus and specificity can be challenging. Finding a clear result requires clear thought. This is why I recommend you establish a weekly pattern of holding a "**Result Hour.**"

Your Result Hour is a period in your schedule each week to sit down and do nothing but think about your result and how you want to achieve it. Don't just schedule this time; protect it. If you do not, you risk falling into the trap of being busy. You'll simply find yourself moving and expending energy without any hope of an upward trajectory.

How is the Result Hour different than traditional time management, or even weekly planning? This is best understood by recognizing the difference between *tactics* and *strategy*. Tactics are the nuts and bolts of doing something. How to win each day by completing and succeeding in micro-tasks such as email or voicemails. Tactics are essential, which is why I teach them in *Time Management Fundamentals*—a

LinkedIn Learning Video course which, to date, has nearly ten million views.[1]

The Result Hour is less about tactics, and more about strategy. Imagine you're a military general in the field of battle trying to stay one swift move ahead, thinking about the bigger picture, and deciding when and where to engage the enemy.

During your Result Hour, you want to immerse yourself in the strategic thinking of defining the result you want. We do this through a series of questions.

Use this chapter to delve into and understand each of these essential, strategic questions. You can also find a helpful worksheet called "The Result Formula" in the appendix of this book that'll guide your thinking… and writing…as you explore these concepts.

---

1. New subscribers to LinkedIn Learning can get a free trial of this course at DaveCrenshaw.com/Time.

QUESTION 1: WHAT DOES A SUCCESSFUL RESULT LOOK LIKE?

How do we know we've reached our destination, unless we've determined our destination in advance? To do this, we must define what success looks like—not in a holistic kind of way, but specifically pertaining to this one result.

If you get your result, what changes? What do you have that you didn't have before? A raise in your hourly income? A better marriage? More return customers? A little less love in your love handles?

Take a moment to write down your answer, either in the worksheet from the appendix or below.

What does a successful result look like?

_____

_____

_____

QUESTION 2: WHAT ARE THE NUMBERS?

Next, let's define the numbers we'll use to measure a successful result. It's hard to get your result without knowing the fine details. After all, you wouldn't sign a five-year contract without knowing if it will be worth it, right? To do this, you'll want to have a clear number in mind.

Suppose you're making $10 per hour and want to increase your take-home pay. Perhaps the next reasonable step up from $10 would be $12 per hour. This is a quantifiable, reasonable result to aim for.

Notice I didn't double or triple our result. When defining the result, we want to think incrementally. One of the reasons people lose their sense of motivation is because they establish unrealistic results. They've given themselves two months to lose forty pounds, which is doomed to fail—if it doesn't kill them first.

Earning money and losing weight are easy to define numerically, since they are numbers-based results. So, how do you put a number value on something as abstract as a relationship with a spouse?

In this case, you'll want to devise something of an arbitrary scale. Think of yourself like a focus group taste-tester and you must rate something with utmost honesty. By rating your relationship on a scale of 0-10, you'll have something quantifiable to assess.

Take a moment to write down your answer, either in the worksheet from the appendix or below.

What are the numbers (that define the result)?

_____

_____

_____

QUESTION 3: WHAT WILL YOU FEEL?

When trying to make improvements in their life, many people fail to give proper attention to their emotions. If you feel no happiness or joy or relief or anything positive from getting a new result, what's the point of the effort? Think about the major life choices you've made up to this point. They've almost all been driven by an intense emotion…or the desire to experience one.

If you're going to stay motivated and focused to get this result, you must get clear about the emotion. Look, you don't have to play the lute and recite poetry in iambic pentameter from memory. Simply write, "I will feel happier when I get this result."

Take a moment to write down your answer, either in the worksheet from the appendix or below.

What will I feel (when I get the result)?

_____

_____

_____

QUESTION 4: WHAT WILL OTHERS FEEL?

This next question pertains to those around you. Getting your result doesn't happen in a vacuum. We must think about how this result will impact others. This is more than just your family. This could mean your coworkers, your customers, your students, and any other people who will be impacted by you getting this result. We want to define what emotion we're setting out to accomplish.

If I'm trying to boost customer loyalty by 10 percent, then I might say I want them to feel like they are part of our family, like they are at home. In fact, this result is one that came from a client of mine—an owner of an auto repair shop.

Note that we again placed a focus on emotion. This is critical, because just in the same way that you are driven by emotion, the people around you, the people who will support you, the people who you want to help will also respond best if the result has an emotional aspect to it. You'll likely need their support to get the result. Having *their* emotions in mind will make it easier for you to enlist their aid.

Take a moment to write down your answer, either in the worksheet from the appendix or below.

What will others feel (when I get the result)?

_____

_____

_____

QUESTION 5: WHY DOES THE RESULT MATTER TO THE RESULT-GETTER(S)?

When asked the question, "Why does this matter?" the question people tend to hear is, "Why does this matter to *me*?" Asking "What's in it for me?" during a job interview is inappropriate. But asking yourself this question inside the quiet sanctuary of your Result Hour is perfectly appropriate and encouraged. However, you're likely going to need the help of others to get this result, so we need to consider their motives as well.

For simplicity, I refer to anyone who's involved in getting a result as the *Result-Get-*

ter, or RG. If you're the only one involved in the process, then the RG is you. But often, there are multiple RGs working together to get the result. This is especially true for organizational results. So, if you're trying to better your organization or need the help of others, you must also think in terms of "What's in it for *them*?"

If I ask my team to do something to get a result, I need to think about their personal self-interest. In my years of coaching, I've discovered the stark truth that few employees truly care about the company they work for. They care about themselves…mostly. I've found this to be true even in organizations with the most altruistic, save-the-world kinds of motives. Even the most socially aware companies have employees motivated by "What have you done for me lately?"

Rather than fight this natural tendency toward self-interest, we're going to acknowledge it and *give back* to those who will give us their time and effort to get the result. I've found getting a new result matters to organizational RGs in one of three ways:

1. The result will help them make more money. AND/OR

2. The result will help make their job easier. AND/OR

3. The result will help make their job more enjoyable.

Take a moment to write down your answer, either in the worksheet from the appendix or below.

Why does the result matter to the Result-Getter(s)?

_____

_____

_____

QUESTION 6: WHEN DO YOU NEED TO ACHIEVE THIS RESULT?

This last question deals with timing. Defining the "due date" of the result is critical, because it helps us keep our expectations realistic. For example, let's say that I determine the result I want to have is $1 million in the bank and I have $10,000 right now. If I say that I want to accomplish this result within one year, I am creating a dangerous expectation. Could it be done? Well, maybe. However, that's the equivalent of saying that Micronesia is going to win next year's FIFA World Cup…without any goals scored against them. Such an irrational expectation will require an even more irrational game plan.

If, however, I said that I want to have $1 million in the bank *ten years* from now, that changes things. It affords me a little more flexibility. I can use my time judiciously, and it does not force me to focus on one result to the exclusion of all others. If I focus entirely on filling my bank account but neglect my family, friends, fitness, and general sense of well-being, then I'm getting one result at the expense of many others.

I have a little mantra that my clients hear me preach regularly. When any of them read this book, they'll have a good chuckle. Anyway, here it goes:

IMPATIENCE IS THE ENEMY OF SUCCESS.

Be patient. Give yourself time to get this result—a realistic amount of time—and not only will you achieve it, but you will feel more balanced in the process.

Take a moment to write down your answer, either in the worksheet from the appendix or below.

When do I need to achieve this result?

_____

_____

_____

A SPECIFIC RESULT

Now that we've outlined how to define our result, take a moment. Because of that tendency toward busy-ness so many of us experience, odds are you haven't yet written answers to any of the questions above. That's natural. Yet doing what is natural and easy keeps us in stasis. Only focused effort will lead to the result we want.

So, slow down. Stop. Take it in. Ponder. Decide.

Then, write it down.

Take ten to fifteen minutes to answer the questions I've outlined above. Once you've done that, you're ready to move on to the next chapter.

CHAPTER 3

The Formula

Now that we've defined the glorious wish you want the genie to grant you (you did that, right?), let's figure out how to get there. Except instead of "wishing on a star" or "dreaming the impossible dream," we're going to use a formula. Before I share that formula, how about a little context?

I began my coaching career at the age of twenty-three in 1998. I was young, foolish, and a tad bit arrogant to think that an inexperienced college student could help business leaders become successful. In the beginning, I relied on a certification program to give me a framework to coach people as well as a bit of street cred. That framework was, essentially, a system. Give people a step-by-step system to follow, and they'll get what they want. "The system is the solution," I was taught, and I taught the same to others.

Over time, I learned that this perspective, while well-intentioned, was fairly limiting. It missed the heart and soul of achieving meaningful results. It wasn't long before I got to work on a philosophy. It grew over the years and, frankly, will continue to develop as long as I'm breathing. [2]

If you are familiar with my past work, specifically *The Focused Business*, you know I referred to this system as "the SAM cycle." While SAM's structure remains steady, I've modified and refined it after years of field experience working with leaders all over the world. I'm so excited to share the best advice I can to get the result you've been looking for.

Without further ado, let's take a look at the Result Formula!

---

2. Expect a 3.0 version of this system to be made available for your VR contact lenses in the coming years.

$$S + A + M = \text{🜃}$$

That's it! But what does "it" mean? Well, first, the flask icon represents the **Result**. It's the result you defined for yourself in the last chapter.

Letter "S" stands for the element of **Systems**, which is a process or procedure someone must follow to get their result.

Letter "A" stands for the element of **Account-ability**, or making yourself accountable to a third party. This is someone who can guide you through the process of getting your result.

Letter "M" stands for the element of **Motivation**. This is far deeper than an after-school special or a "Hang in there, Baby" poster. It's the internal drive you already possess, and we need to connect that drive to the result.

All this brings us back to the Result Formula worksheet I mentioned in the appendix. This is your indispensable tool to using the formula, with blank spaces for you to use any time during your Result Hour.

The steps to use this formula and worksheet are as follows:

1. Define the result in the first column.

2. Analyze what you're missing in terms of the three elements:

   a. Systems

   b. Accountability

   c. Motivation

3. Choose one next action step to take.

4. Gather and process that action on your calendar.[3]

5. Take that action step when the time arrives.

6. Repeat until the result is achieved.

That's it!

---

3. Per my *Time Management Fundamentals* program on LinkedIn Learning. Free trial at DaveCrenshaw.com/Time.

This formula is simple. Yes, it requires effort—but don't let that discourage you. In fact, part of the magic of the formula is how it helps you keep moving forward by removing the burden of figuring everything out upfront. Thinking too much about all the work is what gets most people stuck in the mire of negative procrastination. Instead, focus on *just the next step* you decide to take with the help of the formula. Ignore everything else.

In this way, many small achievements connect together to create one very big result!

You may be a little skeptical about this formula, and that's okay. Let me illustrate, in shorthand, how powerful it can be and how each element plays a crucial role.

The power of SAM is best illustrated by considering broken versions of the formula. Let's imagine one element is missing…

$$S + A + (M \times O) = Compliance$$

Looks like algebra, doesn't it? I promise it's simpler than it may look. You probably recognized (S)ystems and (A)ccountability. What about this "M x 0" stuff? Well, that just means Motivation is missing. It's a situation where someone is trying to get a result they don't really care about.

Without a connection to internal motivation, you're going to see people just following the rules without any emotional heft added to the equation. These folks just go through the motions, acting as if they are on the verge of reaching the mountaintop, but really they're just being compliant. Their heart just isn't in it.

Let's imagine Bob. Bob says he needs to lose weight. He finds a system to follow. He hits the gym every day. He buys protein shakes and compression wear. He even goes to a personal trainer, who holds him accountable. But, given the first opportunity or excuse to give up, Bob rebounds back to his previous state. Why? Because all that effort wasn't attached to a truly meaningful motivator.

Let's look at this from a different angle. What happens when we zero-out Accountability?

$$S + (A \times O) + M = Decline$$

This, as you may have guessed, is someone who lacks Accountability. In this new version of the formula, Bob didn't make the investment to get a personal trainer or even just find an exercise buddy. Bob did the research and found a system he believes in, and he's got some very personal, very deep reasons that drive him to make the change. But he's a DIYer. Why get a personal trainer when you can just watch some weightlifting videos on YouTube?

Bob gets excited about how his glutes are going to look after doing squats. His motivation is high in early January, after creating a New Year's resolution. But in February, the commitment of the new year seems like a distant memory. There's no one to report to. Over time, it all starts to fall apart, and both Systems and Motivation begin to fall into disarray. Why? Because there's no person outside of Bob holding him accountable, checking his form, keeping things fresh, and maintaining his focus on the path to his result. A lack of Accountability perpetuates an abundance of forgetfulness.

Time to consider the last broken equation…

$$(S \times O) + A + M = Inconsistency$$

When you don't have Systems to follow, you're on the fast track to disaster. Bob might be pumped to pump that iron and make himself accountable to a friend. Without a system, though, he's making things up every single time he steps into the gym with his buddy. We're here! Time to work out!

Then Bob wanders from weight rack to weight rack, machine to machine, blindly picking things up and lifting with his back. Before long, he finds himself in the emergency room with a strained groin, forced to spend the next ten weeks on the couch. What he needs is a path to follow.

Can you see how you can quickly diagnose what you—or your friend Bob—are missing simply by looking at the results you are getting? There are other breakdowns, as well. Occasionally, a person lacks more than one element. Others have all three elements in place, but haven't taken the time to clearly define a focused, specific result. The point is that the Result Formula can help you quickly diagnose what isn't working and guide you toward correcting the problem.

Now, let's pause for a moment. I just gave you the secret sauce. It's what I've been selling to my clients for the last twenty years. My clients pay *thousands* of dollars for this advice, and you're getting it for next-to-nothing. Why would I give such valuable knowledge away?

Well, I have a result in mind. For me, it's personal. I want to start a movement. Not a creepy-cult-leader kind of movement, but a movement of hundreds of thousands of people getting the result they want. The idea of you getting your result is deeply motivational to me. Why? Because my whole career has been built upon the principle that when others succeed, I succeed too.

That's where you come in. I need your help, and the help you can give me is by first helping yourself. Continue reading and following the Result Formula. Get the result you want. Prove that it works through your own actions. When you get your result, let me know at result@DaveCrenshaw.com.

Then, tell others about it. Share this book. Provide accountability to someone to help them get *their* result.

Someday, I may create my own certification program to help you help others get their result...much in the same way I got my start as a skinny, cocky, 23-year-old. Maybe, maybe not. Either way, you can still share this book.

Help yourself, then help others.

I hope that you become so adept at this that you can use this formula whenever you see something you wish to improve in your life, organization, or career. Your thought process will instantly jump to:

$$S + A + M = $$

The following chapters will cover the three major steps of the formula, beginning with those Systems I mentioned!

CHAPTER 4

Systems

So, what is this "System" thing I've been yammering about? It might sound like a corporate buzzword, yet it has a very deep, powerful purpose. You may know it by process, flow chart, diagram, or checklist. In the end, a system is just a procedure for getting an intended result. Think of it like a cookbook or a manual to install furniture from Ikea.

All of us are surrounded by systems. We abide by traffic codes, wait in line at the grocery store, and even go to bed according to a system.

Systems are sometimes easier to identify at the organizational level. Whenever you grab a bite at a fast food chain, the people preparing your food follow a tightly-wound system in order to get you a consistent Big N'

Tasty. They probably have a system in place for telling you that the milkshake machine is out too!

Most intuitively understand the value of a system because, essentially, human beings are the stuff of systems. Our bodies are highly calibrated machines made of parts that interact with other parts from our brain to our liver, from our heart to our bones, from our lungs to our spleen. Our bodily systems are built to keep us alive and kicking. Systems are so critical to our survival that if one organ breaks down and fails to operate, the whole system can shut down.

Similarly, if we're trying to achieve the result, we must use a system. Not just any system—a proven system.

The result formula element of Systems—like the elements of Accountability and Motivation—is made up of three other elements. I'll call them "sub-elements." For Systems, the sub-elements are:

Who + How + With What = System

WHO

So, let's talk about "who." No, not the classic rock band or the people of Whoville. The first aspect of a system is the person following it. No matter how powerful a system is, if a person cannot execute it, they will never achieve a consistent result. We must be realistic.

My field experience has taught me that getting the result begins with a simple question: "Do we have the right person to get this result?"

There's no shame in saying no. We all must give hard "no's" for expectations that are unrealistic. I mentioned this earlier example: If I am only five-two and the result that I'm trying to get is to become an NBA center, my chances of getting my result are absurdly infinitesimal. Nonexistent, really. No matter how skilled I become at basketball, I simply do not have the needed traits.

Remember this rule: Traits cannot be taught, while skills can.

Skills are acquired knowledge. Traits are *who you are*, speaking both physically and psychologically.

A trait is something you were born with, that you came into this world knowing how to do. For instance, many people are born with the trait of being outgoing, but other people are born with the trait of being more analytical and just can't grasp the idea of becoming the life of the party.

Yet, when I talk to leaders of organizations about their hiring processes, they focus all too often on people with excellent skills. They open a resume and see an undergrad MBA from this college, five years at that company, and a mentor from so-and-so at some fancy conglomerate.

While skills have value, they could be considered secondary to traits. Why? Because you can teach skills over time. Teaching traits is…well, like trying to teach someone who is five feet two inches to be taller.

Which brings us back to our opening question: "Who?" When looking at the result you're trying to accomplish, ask: "Do the Result-Getters possess the necessary traits for accomplishing this?" If not, I'm not going to be able to accomplish it. Because, whether we like it or not, we are governed by laws of physics, nature, space, and time… just to name a few.

Yes, I know there are truly motivational stories about people who overcame extreme physical limitations to accomplish remarkable things. But if you look at what they accomplished, it was still within the realm of possible reality—not delusional fantasy.

So, if you've jumped out of the gate lacking a required trait, it may be time to reassess your targeted result. Make adjustments so that what you seek to accomplish is reasonable, given what nature has given you. It's time to go back to square one knowing what your limits will have to be.

And, if you're trying to get an organizational result and you're about to hire the kind of person with all the right skills and all the wrong traits, do not send that offer letter. Say thanks but no thanks, and move on to the next candidate. Better to hire someone inexperienced who you can teach, than someone you can never transform into something they are not.

HOW

"How" is the first word most think of when asked to define a system. They ask, "How do I do it?" In its most basic form, "how" is just an instruction manual. When asked to do laundry, I have a system in place:

- Step 1. Laundry day arrives.
- Step 2. Collect my clothes.
- Step 3. Place clothes in washer.
- Step 4. Add detergent.
- Step 5. Spin the knob on the washer and basically guess where the dial should be.
- Step 6. Move to the dryer.

- Step 7. Add dryer sheet.

- Step 8. Again, take a shot in the dark to turn on the dryer.

- Step 9. Buzzer goes off. Clothes still wet. Send it through another dry cycle.

- Step 10. Buy a new dryer.

Okay, so maybe that's a poor system, but you get the idea. The "how" is simply a collection of predefined, documented steps strung together to achieve a result.

But if we haven't ever achieved a result before, and don't have a system, where should we start? The easiest way is to look for others who got that result and find out what process they followed.

Let's suppose I wanted to write a book. I'd ask other people who have written a book about their process. How did they get it done? Of course, there are thousands of ways to write a book. I can't expect Dean Koontz to have the same book-writing method that I do. Does that mean his way is wrong? No, it just means that I have found a system that works for me.

Keep this maxim in mind:

THERE IS NO SUCH THING AS A PERFECT SYSTEM. THERE IS ONLY THE NEXT DRAFT.

Because this is a true principle, start with *something*. Any system will do, really. Try it and write it out. Documentation is critical because our memory is fallible. We tend to forget things that are just rattling around in our brain. An undocumented system is no system at all. To help you create your first draft, in the appendix you'll find a blank System Template to help guide your system creation.

Allow me to share a couple of final tips about the "how." First, the first step is always the **trigger event** or an inciting incident. Find an event that tells you it is time to use your system. For example, a business system for greeting customers is initiated when a customer walks through the door. In the laundry example above, the trigger event is that the scheduled laundry day arrives.

Second, give ample attention to your traits when creating your system. Don't fight them; use them to your advantage. For instance, in my effort to be more physically fit, I have learned that I personally just don't do well with free weights. Something about all the attention they require just triggers my ADHD in a "Holy cow, I want to die!" way...after just two reps. However, I do quite well with machines. Why? Because it feels like a game to me. Experts might say I'd get better results with free weights, and they'd have charts and graphs to prove their point. The problem is that, if I'm being honest, it's machines or nothing.

Better to make progress with an imperfect system than to try using a "perfect" system you'll never follow. You can always come back later and improve it.

WITH WHAT

This brings us to "with what," which refers to the tools or objects we need to complete our system and get our result. We may have our cookie recipe at the ready, yet we also need flour, a cookie sheet, and a host of other do-dads to create some chewy goodness. In our exercise example, the tools were the workout equipment...not to mention some appropriate exercise clothes.

Proper tools are crucial. This is the "investing in our future" that we always hear about from corporate talking heads. For instance, what kind of computer do you use? How about your monitor? Is your keyboard ergonomic? Is your photo editing software up to date?

If you want to improve yourself, you'll need to spend money on yourself. Don't wait for your company or manager to determine whether it's okay to get an upgraded keyboard...well, maybe if you have a finicky and vengeful IT department. Otherwise, invest in yourself.

But "with what" is more than just physical, mechanical, or digital tools. It can be something like food. If you find yourself buying a sleeve of Oreos every day, that's going to minimize your chances of successfully getting your result. The investment there may be in healthier snack. Or a water bottle. Whatever you need to help you get the result, get it. Get the best you can afford, because it will pay for itself many times over in the long run.

WRAPPING UP

Now that we've covered the three sub-elements of Systems, make some notes in the Result Formula worksheet. Ask what you have and what you're missing.

Then, ask yourself, "Which of the three sub-elements—Who, How, or With What—do I need to improve?" Should you improve your skills? Are you missing traits and, if so, do you need to re-adjust your target result? When can you take time to document a system? Do you need to invest in the proper tools to help you get that result?

Make note of any potential areas for improvement.

After you analyze that step, it's time to move on to the next element of the Result Formula: Accountability.

CHAPTER 5

Accountability

As you move closer to your result, you're going to find that Accountability is essential. As powerful as it is and as often as we hear it, few people know what true accountability is. This is because people use a very loose definition of the word.

You hear people use self-help catchphrases like, "I can be accountable to myself." However, that phrase misses the power of true accountability. That's just "responsibility"—which, don't get me wrong, is something I encourage. However, I've found in coaching leaders around the world that responsibility and discipline do little to get people closer to their result.

In truth, many of my most successful clients lack responsibility. I'd go so far as to say

I'm a pretty undisciplined person. What has worked for us is not some grand work ethic. What has worked for us is making ourselves accountable to *others*, thus becoming the products of great coaching.

Conversely, I've seen many people who hold themselves up as "experts" repeatedly violate their own teaching. Because they feel that they have enough knowledge and experience that they no longer need to answer to anyone else, they drift off course. Responsibility without accountability is a recipe for hypocrisy.

To make myself abundantly clear, accountability requires a third party. This third party is at least one brain other than your own influencing your behavior. Responsibility is how well you follow through on the things you've committed to, using your own willpower. But we're all human, and it's human nature to be forgetful, make excuses, and go astray. Accountability takes over when responsibility fails you.

This brings up the question: To whom should I make myself accountable? Well, in my view, there are three major archetypes that offer you accountability.

1. **The Coach:** This is an individual who has been hired or trained to help get other people their result. They could be certified, or they could just be successful in the field of helping others. What matters most is their success rate. Often, the most successful people I've met work with multiple coaches. They'll have a health coach, a life coach, a marketing coach, a communication coach. If you invest in a good coach, you might see an amazing return.

2. **The Mentor:** They may not have any special certification. They may not be taking money for their services. They might not even be in the same industry. Yet, they've seen it all! More importantly, they've already achieved the result you're trying to get. Rather than being a teacher, they can show you the

way of things. They know the mistakes they made and can convey those mistakes to you. Mentors offer a fresh set of eyes to help you sort out your problems.

3. **The Supervisor:** Great managers straddle the line between coach and mentor. They are paid for their services, but they are paid because they can get results out of those they manage. They have a delegated responsibility to hold you accountable. One drawback, however, is that their allegiances may be toward the organization more than the individual.

You may have noticed some people in your life are missing from this shortlist. That's on purpose. You love your friends and your family—and that's exactly why they don't belong on this list. Why? We'll get to that shortly. However, for now, know that your target is to get the *result*. The best way to get that result is by relying on those who are experts at holding people accountable.

So, what sub-elements make up Accountability?

Trust + Training + Follow-Up = Accountability

TRUST

Trust is your confidence in another's ability to get you the result you're trying to achieve. We must feel confident in the coach, mentor, or supervisor we've selected. It's crucial that we know they have our best interests at heart and know the pathway to get us there.

There is no phrase that irks me to my core quite like this aphorism:

THOSE WHO CAN, DO; THOSE WHO CAN'T, TEACH.

Is there truth to this statement? Well, perhaps. It's like saying your high school gym coach couldn't make it as an all-state quarterback, so he took a teaching job instead. That said, it implies those who teach do not create value. But teachers and coaches themselves, in fact, have incredible value.

Michael Phelps, the greatest Olympic athlete of all time, works with some guy named Bob

Bowman. Why? Well, it's not because he forgets how to swim. It's not because he doesn't have the natural traits of a godlike swimmer. It's because he understands the power of accountability.

Often, I've found that people who are focused on their greatest strength have significant blind spots. This creates an opportunity for improvement. A great teacher sees these blind spots in a way the individual can't, and helps the competitor in business, life, or even swimming get the result they're looking for.

You must work with someone who has either achieved the result you're trying to get or is gifted at helping people achieve it. Coaches are often better than mentors at helping people get their results, because they specialize in the success of *others*. However, mentors also can add great value, due to their experience.

Just make sure you team up with someone who can get you where you're trying to go. One of the biggest mistakes people make, not just in getting a result but in life in general, is surrounding themselves with people who have achieved very little. The bigger mistake is listening to those people.

One of the turning points of my career was when I noticed the people who surrounded me had hardly accomplished anything. I made a conscious decision to change my inner circle. I began associating with people who were truly successful and lived balanced lives. It made all the difference in my career.

Make yourself accountable to people you trust to help you get your result.

TRAINING

Working with a coach or mentor is more than simply getting together for lunch once in a while to talk about what's going on. No, you and those who you are accountable to must train hands-on on a regular basis. Also, keep in mind that if you're trying to get an organizational result, it's likely *you'll* need to be the one providing training from time to time, as well.

In my view, training revolves around a single word: repetition. Repetition helps us hone and improve small skills, yet many people are afraid of it. Repetition becomes easier over time, yet many people aren't willing to do something over and over and over again. Repetition is a powerful teacher, yet it is the most underutilized method of self-improvement.

You may notice occasionally throughout this book that I repeat myself. Repeat myself. Repeat myself…sorry, got caught in another repetition loop.

In my online courses, some of the feedback I get is, "He repeats himself too much." When someone says that, I know they have not yet learned the power repetition has to get results.

If you've ever played a sport or a musical instrument, you know how important repetition is. For instance, when I was learning how to play volleyball, my coach informed me that my form was all wrong. Not just how I served the ball, but pretty much everything. I needed to improve from top to bottom: new footwork, new upper body mechanics, new ways of holding my hands. It wasn't easy. These weren't natural positions for me to stand in, and I started to tense up. My coach, unrelenting, didn't give me an alternative stance. He made me repeat my stance over and over until, eventually, it became comfortable.

Concert pianists achieve a master's level of dexterity through constant training and repetition of their craft. The best teachers drill them continually, and demand perfection. They create perfect performance through perfect repetition.

When you see top performers make something "look effortless," they do so because of repetition. Jerry Seinfeld said that he performed his entire act on small stages in New York at least 200 times before he made his 1981 *Tonight Show* debut with a tight, five-minute set. This five-minute moment completely altered the course of his career.

Why? Because, not only was it funny—he also made it look effortless.

We understand this principle for entertainers and athletes. Yet for some reason, in the business world, we expect immediate gratification from the folks we manage or employ. When we want people to improve their behavior, we show them how to do it once, maybe twice. When they don't do it perfectly the next time? Well, we complain. We may even give them, "It's not you, it's me." Then, we write them up and eventually tell them to hit the bricks.

But how do we create meaningful repetition? The process I've taught to my coaching clients is "demonstrate, practice, observe."

Demonstrate means showing someone how something should be done. You model it perfectly. As you demonstrate, you say, "This is how I'm holding my hands. This is how I'm moving my feet. This is the word I use to greet my customers. This is how I use the machine."

Next, **practice**. Time to switch roles and pass the torch to the person being trained. They attempt to perform that task the way you demonstrated. As they're practicing, the coach gives feedback and says, "Make this adjustment. Watch out for this."

Finally, **observe**. The coach says nothing, sits back, and watches the person attempt to complete this task. After they complete the task, it's time for a couple items of feedback. Repeat. Repeat again.

Once it gets enough reps, the task becomes second nature and comfortable for the person to do that system properly. We must make repetitive training a priority.

This, of course, begs a question: Is your training schedule with your coach or mentor calendared? Is there a structure in place for repetition?

FOLLOW-UP

The last sub-element of Accountability is follow-up. It isn't enough to do what we're supposed to do. English mathematician

Karl Pearson has been credited with the following statement: "That which is measured improves. That which is measured and reported improves exponentially."

Follow-up is the way in which you gauge, and maintain, your accountability. The measurement takes place between the coach and you. The coach needs to check with you to see how you're doing on a regular basis. My physical fitness coach checks in with me through measurements—not just weight, but body fat percentage and body part measurement as well. This ongoing return and report keeps me focused and following the system...even when I don't want to do it.

The clients I've worked with personally report to me on a weekly basis about their time management numbers. Conversely, I report to my business coach on a weekly basis with the exact same numbers. Just because I'm an expert doesn't mean I don't need accountability. Therapists need therapists, doctors need doctors, and everyone needs accountability.

There are a couple of ways your coach or mentor can follow up with you. First is through an email report, such as an automatic report that goes out weekly. To keep things simple, it's best to limit the report to a few questions. Even better, make this reporting numbers-based. The more detailed reporting becomes, the less likely people are to do it. Keep it simple.

Additionally, there should be in-person reporting—typically on a monthly or semi-monthly basis. This can take place via phone, video conference, or in-person. This is an opportunity to measure, personally discuss progress, and, of course, receive training.

Whatever you decide, make sure you and your accountability partner have mutually agreed upon a clear pattern of follow-up.

WRAPPING UP

Now that we've covered the three elements of Accountability, make some notes in the Result Formula worksheet. Ask what you have and what you're missing.

Then, ask yourself, "Which of the three sub-elements—Trust, Training, or Follow-up—do I need to improve?" Have you clearly identified and enlisted the help of a coach, mentor, or supervisor you trust? Are you receiving training on a consistent basis? Is the training meaningful and repetitive? Do you have a pattern for consistent follow-up and reporting of progress?

Make note of any potential areas for improvement.

Now, we're ready to move to the last element in the Result Formula: Motivation.

CHAPTER 6:

Motivation

The third and final element in our Result Formula is Motivation.

It's hard to look at a word like motivation and *not* think about anything other than Chris Farley as Matt Foley, the motivational speaker. Think about motivation long enough, and you can see him hitching up his pants and living in a van down by the river. You might even envision a 90s motivational poster preaching "Teamwork makes the dream work."

The word "motivation" can be easily ridiculed and satirized because the world has an endless supply of useful idiots motivating us into indifference. They preach a motivation that comes from outside yourself. Yet no one—not me or anyone else—can tell you what you need, how to feel, or what drives you. That comes from within.

Motivation doesn't have to be such a cringe-worthy word. After all, everyone is motivated by something. The only question is, by what? You may be motivated to get a paycheck and long for early retirement. Others may be motivated by their next cheap thrill, maybe a dangerous narcotic. I may be motivated to play video games for hours on end. Motivation isn't something we acquire; it's an ever-present passenger, riding on our backs and pushing us toward one action or another.

What is lacking, then, is not motivation itself—but, rather, awareness of mental and emotional *connection* to that motivation. Only a handful of us see the connection between our actions and dreams. Few of us have made the jump from where we want to go and what we're doing in the present. That's where we tend to break down.

We're disconnected from what motivates us. We may not even be sure what is motivating us. For years, I knew that I needed exercise, but did nothing about it. I made efforts to start. However, like so many of us, each time I took a step up, I fell two steps behind.

There's a metaphorical dusty Stairmaster in everyone's basement. We all know that we need to go downstairs and use it, but that doesn't even complete step one. To motivate ourselves, we must understand what our real desire is and why taking action matters at all.

What got me exercising in my metaphorical—and somewhat literal—dusty basement wasn't a desire to lower my blood pressure or run in a 5K charity event. I had to ask myself what it was that was really driving me. What did I *actually* care about? In this case, getting physically fit was less about health and more about—well, just looking good...looking *better*, at least.

I spend a lot of time on camera and am a part of the editing process. After a while, you start to get self-critical. While I'm happy being who I am, I wanted to look strong, healthy, and energetic for my online students. It was a *realistic* result. It was never my goal to get cast in the next *Magic Mike* movie. I just wanted to look better.

Whatever result *you* want to achieve, you must also make a connection between what you want most, your internal motivation, and the actions you must take today to get you there. So, what makes you want to take action? Connecting to your pre-existing motivation requires us to look at three sub-elements. This formula is:

Values + Vision + Cause = Motivation

VALUES

In general, what do you *believe* in? What gets you up in the morning? Why do you do or not do things for others? What brought you to your work, your family, your friends, your lifestyle?

Many of us seemingly do things blindly. Yet, if you slow down and take a magnifying glass to your actions, you'll realize that somewhere along the line, a value—something you believe in—drove you to them. So, take a look at what you do and why you do it. The better you understand your current value system, the better you'll be able to connect the result to that system one way or another.

For instance, let's say you're in the market for a career upgrade. You're seeking a better job than you have right now. Ask yourself *what value is driving this action*—in this case, searching for a new job.

It may seem obvious. After all, I pretty much state a motive in the premise: a better job. However, think about the bigger picture. In the grand scheme of things, why does this matter to you? Why does it matter at all?

Perhaps you hate being watched, and the job you seek offers you more autonomy?

Write that down, and ask again, "Why does autonomy matter to me?"

Maybe you've got a kind soul, and want to serve?

Write that down, and ask again, "Why does service matter to me?"

Is it the ability to impact others? Do you want more influence or notoriety?

Write that down, and ask again, "Why does influence matter to me?"

Whatever comes to mind, write those statements down. Keep digging until you can't go any deeper. Your answers to these kinds of questions are the beginning sparks of crafting powerful, motivating values.

Values are simple statements distilled into short phrases or sentences. It's not a mission statement or a vision board. Instead, think of three to ten words or phrases that sum up what you believe in.

In an organizational setting, values are often documented as "core values." One notable example is the company values at Zappos. These are ten values that Tony Hsieh and his team created to summarize what makes Zappos unique, and why those values are meaningful to employees.

One of my favorites Zappos values is: "Create fun and a little weirdness." It's so distinct. Most large companies look at "weirdness" and fear it as being childish. That's their loss, not Zappos'.

Alternatively, "being safe" is an equally valid value that you, or any organization, could also espouse. The question of values is much less about being unique, and more about identifying what is truly meaningful to you or your organization.

So, this sub-element of values has two potential flavors: your *personal* values and, if you work for an organization, the *organizational* values. While these often differ from each other, the ideal situation—and the most motivational one—is where the two different values harmonize with each other. The people who work in a company that aligns with their values are the happiest.

So, for a moment, just answer this one question: What is something that you value? What motivates your actions every day? Take a moment to write that down. If you've never created values before, start with an imperfect first draft. Over time, you can revisit your values to refine them into a motivational masterpiece.

Once you have a first draft of your values, make the motivational connection. Ask yourself, "Why do my values drive me to get this result?"

VISION

In the beginning of this book, the single result you created was an intermediate step. A short-term accomplishment. Where is this all going? Toward accomplishing your long-term vision.

Vision is your big picture. This is the castle in the clouds. It's the happiest destination for your life that you could possibly imagine.

Think of the vision this way: If you're driving from LA to New York, an intermediate step might be to stop in Las Vegas. As nice—and distracting—as Vegas might be, it's not the destination. We must keep moving forward, rather than getting stuck in an illusory world of Elvis impersonators and slot machines. So, we must get on the road again toward the next stop.

We must never forget the ultimate destination. The vision helps us maintain forward momentum.

A healthy vision always includes a "when"—a timeframe. I've found a span of about five years is a healthy timetable for most visions. Ask yourself, "Where do I want to be in five years?" Avoid the cheesy answer you may have given at a job interview. You're not answering to your employer, your spouse, your coworkers, or me. This is about you, and there's no right or wrong answer. Be real. Be honest. Frankly, don't be afraid to think selfishly for now.

Where do you intend to be five years from now? Think about it and write it down. Keep it short. Your final vision shouldn't be more than a page, so don't feel the need to wax eloquent...unless "waxing eloquent" is one of your values, of course.

If you need help structuring your response, think in terms of "be," "do," and "have":

- Who do I want to BE five years from now?

- What will I DO five years from now?

- What will I HAVE five years from now?

Once you've answered these questions and created a rough five-year vision, make the connection to the result you're going to get. Ask yourself, "How does this result tie into my five-year vision?"

CAUSE

Many of the clients I work with want more "buy-in" from their employees. They explore something like profit-sharing. The theory is that if you monetize effort, people will be incentivized to work harder. Who wouldn't like to make more money, right? And if doing X gives people more cash, then, logically, they'll be driven to do more of X, right?

Not always. Far less than you might think, in fact.

While it sounds nice in practice, monetization is a surprisingly limited motivator. It is absolutely true that, organizationally speaking, employers must take care of basic human needs. Once their basic needs are satisfied, however, people are driven by something much deeper. This is where *cause* comes in.

First, allow me to explain why this is true. Ever heard of Maslow's Hierarchy of Needs? It's a psychological construct that simplifies explaining what motivates people. The foundations of this pyramid are physiological needs like food and sleep, followed by safety. If you were a Paleolithic bipedal primate hunting and eating squirrels while running away from mastodons, the foundation of your hierarchy of needs was ample food and shelter—but isn't that what a paycheck is, too?

After all, money pays for food and shelter… provided it's sufficient for the needs of the employee and their family. And sufficient pay is necessary. If you have employees who are consistently underpaid, it's going to be very hard for them to be loyal to the company, let alone try to get a new result. This is also true on a personal level. You're likely going to be motivated by money if you feel that you do not have what you need to pay the bills and survive. So, to that degree, money is a valid motivator.

However, once those *essential* needs are taken care of, people are most often motivated by something else. Once we're at a point in which money is less meaningful, we find ourselves looking for a cause.

I find that people are best motivated when they have purpose. This is a larger, perhaps metaphysical idea that is greater than ourselves. It can be to make the world a better place, to rid the world of traffic, to help the homeless, to better protect the environment. For others, it may be motivated by religion.

An individual's cause is as unique as their fingerprint.

What cause is meaningful to you?

One of my favorite causes is Kiva. This organization[4] makes it easy to provide a micro-loan to entrepreneurs all around the world. These are men and women working to create jobs, provide for their families, and make the world a better place. It's not a handout, but a hand up.

Kiva is a cause that speaks to *me*. Why? Because I believe in the cause of entrepreneurship. Not just social entrepreneurship, but financial, real, for-profit entrepreneurship to change communities and change the world. It creates jobs which, in turn, create security, happiness, and self-confidence.

Kiva not only matters to me; it drives many of the decisions I make in business. I want to succeed so I can support these men and women looking to build something that lasts. It motivates me. I use some of the freedom I've achieved through my success to contribute both time and money to Kiva. It makes me feel good. It makes me want to do

---

4. Visit Kiva.org to learn more.

more. In turn, I want to do even better in my career so I can give and participate more.

My cause may not be your cause, and that's just as it should be! There are many kinds of causes, and they all could use *your* help. Picking one, maybe two, and focusing on them is the best way to not only make a difference, but to *drive* your daily actions and motivate you to improve. You will be more likely to achieve new results in *any* capacity in your life, when you have a cause that is deeply meaningful to you.

Imagine the result you're trying to get is a salary increase, and your cause is panda sanctuaries. If you make the mental and emotional connection that a salary increase helps you donate to those fluffy, cuddly guys, then you will find an extra boost of motivation.

Want a bonus secret—no charge? I've heard executive after executive tell me stories that, when they began to give more of themselves to others, success returned to them, multiplied many times over. Dozens of leaders have told me that whenever they gave, it always came back to them in ways they never expected. I call it the "generosity effect." Whatever you want to call this phenomenon, it's been proven to me many times over that giving time and money to a meaningful cause not only motivates you to achieve more, but becomes a very real catalyst for your success.

So, what cause drives *you*? Think about it.

What is something greater than money that you care about? What are you willing to contribute a portion of your time and money to, when you get the result?

Take a moment to write down your answer to that question. Also, write down an action for yourself to get involved with a compelling cause. If you don't yet know a cause that specifically serves that need, then search for one…or in a small way, start one.

Then, make the connection to the result you're going to get. Ask yourself, "Why will getting my result help me serve this cause?"

WRAPPING UP

Now that we've covered the three elements of Motivation, make some notes in the Result Formula worksheet. Ask what you have and what you're missing.

Then, ask yourself, "Which of the three sub-elements—Values, Vision, or Cause—do I need to improve?" Have you, or your organization, created a written list of defined values? Do you, or your organization, have at least a first draft of a brief five-year vision? Do you have a selfless cause that you serve? Have you connected your values, vision, and cause to the result you're working to get?

Make note of any potential areas for improvement.

You've now reached the end of exploring the Result Formula. You're doing great! In the final chapter, we'll discuss how to make this formula a part of your everyday plan.

CHAPTER 7

Next Steps

We've now outlined everything you need to get the result you want, in any aspect of your personal life, your career, or your organization. But having the formula is not enough. You must take action. The shorter the distance between you gaining knowledge and acting upon it, the more successful you will become.

So, let's talk about some action steps to take to move forward quickly. Think of this as a game plan for executing your game plan.

1. **Schedule your Result Hour.**

   Do you have trouble committing to things when they aren't scheduled? I sure do! The result you're trying to get requires visualization. Rather than just taking an hour here or there, make your Result Hour official with a timeslot on your calendar. Create a recurring appointment with yourself. Commit to yourself—and your accountability leader—that you will keep this time. Let nothing get in your way.

2. **Define your result.**

Your Result Hour is more than you just envisioning a life of sitting next to a swimming pool drinking out of a coconut. It goes deeper than fantasy. As mentioned, it's strategy. As you stand on the field of battle, you need to be aware of the contingencies. Use the Result Formula worksheet I provided in the appendix and answer these questions:

What does a successful result look like? What are the numbers? What will you feel? What will others feel? Why does the result matter to the Result-Getter(s)? When do you need to achieve the result?

3. **Dive deep.**

Take some time to walk through the Result Formula. Answer all the questions under each element. Look for places where Systems, Accountability, and Motivation already exist in your world. Take a closer look for where you could use more SAM.

4. **Choose one action.**

The Result Hour isn't finished until you know which steps to take next. However, for the time being, keep it simple. Select just *one* action you're going to take to move toward the result. Once you know that action, put a reminder for it into an approved gathering point.

5. **Follow your time management system to complete that action.**

What's an "approved gathering point," you may ask? You may have picked up this book without any prior knowledge of my previous work. That's a good thing! It's a sign that *The Result* movement may be gaining traction. Those who have worked with me know all about my approved gathering points. It's a crucial component of my *Time Management* teaching.

You can learn about this in my LinkedIn Learning course Time Management Fundamentals. You can get access to this course by going to DaveCrenshaw.com/Time and grabbing your free trial to LinkedIn Learning. *Time Management Fundamentals* is essential for giving you a framework for following through.

Of course, if you *already* possess a solid time management system that you follow to get everything done—on time, exactly as promised, and with no stress—keep using that system to follow through on your chosen action.

6. **Repeat the Result Formula.**

In earlier chapters, I mentioned that while the steps to get your result may be easy, the process takes effort. This brings us back to our partner in success: *repetition*. Fortunately, the more you repeat, the more strength you build. Repeat the Result Formula as many times as necessary until you get your result.

Because you're only going to be focusing on one action step toward getting the result, it's possible that over time you'll need to take multiple actions. You might need just one. Some of my clients find their result by analyzing, using the formula, and implementing just one of the action steps they discover. The minute they dig in and accomplish one step, the other steps fall like dominoes.

However, if at the end of this process your result is not within arm's reach, simply go back to our handy worksheet. Check high and low for places where SAM might be missing.

Repeat these steps until the result is achieved. Simple? Yes. Easy? No. Patience may be required. The good news is, if you've chosen an accountability leader wisely, they'll help you to continue moving forward.

Now, let's talk about optional steps.

If you're not on my list to receive weekly training, please subscribe at DaveCrenshaw.com. This isn't some self-promotional "buy my stuff" ad that I've smuggled into this book. Rather, this is about getting yourself tied into a support team of tens of thousands of people from around the world. Every week, I'll bring stories, examples, and questions from people like you, and I'll be discussing greater insights into how to achieve the result. The videos that I send out are free, and you're equally free to subscribe or unsubscribe at any time.

Also, I would encourage you to reach out to me on social media. I send updates via LinkedIn, YouTube, and Facebook. Choose your favorite.

While I probably can't become your personal coach,[5] if you find yourself stuck in trying to get your result, need clarification about the Result Formula, or you're unclear

---

5. I currently work with new coaching clients by referral only.

on what you should do next, please submit a video question at DaveCrenshaw.com/Ask. If I think the question will help both you and other people, I will answer it!

Finally, if you haven't already, please share this book with a friend. Send them to GetYourResult.com to get their own copy.

Everyone can use a system for delivering on a happy and successful life. Not only will it help them grow, but it will help you with your result as well. Accomplishments rarely happen in a vacuum. Having a friend by your side doubles your effectiveness. You don't have to be accountable to each other. You just have to be there for each other.

Knowing that someone, anyone, is reading this part of the book fills my heart with joy. I'm grateful that you took the time to get through this. My hope is that it makes your life successful, simpler, and satisfying.

It will require effort, patience, and, yes, some repetition. You didn't pick up this book for an easy answer. But getting through each page tells me that you are committed to improvement. I look forward to hearing about your success.

Now, get to work! You have a result to get!

APPENDIX

THE RESULT FORMULA WORKSHEET

On the next page, you'll see a blank Result Processing Worksheet. Use this during your Result Hour to define your result, analyze, and create action steps. You can print out this document for your own personal use. However, this document is copyrighted material and may not be re-adapted or reused without my written consent.

Use the worksheet as follows:

1. Take time to define your result. Answering each question should take roughly ten to thirty minutes. (Keep in mind that this is copyrighted material and cannot be reused in a book, adapted, or used for professional services without my written permission.)

2. Assess what you already have and what you do not have by looking at each factor in the Result Formula: Systems, Accountability, and Motivation. Complete each section of the worksheet.

3. Choose one action. Although you may be tempted to go all-in, choose one step—the best action—and focus on it until you complete it.

4. Gather that unprocessed action into an approved gathering point, as defined in *Time Management Fundamentals* on LinkedIn Learning.

5. Process that action using What, When, Where processing as defined by *Time Management Fundamentals*.

6. Take action when that time arrives on your calendar.

7. Repeat steps 1-6 until you get your result.

THE RESULT FORMULA by DAVE CRENSHAW

GetYourResult.com

The Result	=	Systems (Who + How + With What)	+	Accountability (Trust + Training + Follow-up)	+	Motivation (Values + Vision + Cause)
What does a successful result look like?		• Do(es) the RG(s) have the necessary traits?		• Has a leader (coach, mentor, or manager) been designated to help the RG(s) get this result?		Does the RG/Organization have meaningful, written values?
What are the numbers?		• Do(es) the RG(s) have the necessary skills?		• Do(es) the RG(s) trust this leader as a guide in getting this result?		Do those values connect to the result? (If so, how?)
What will you feel?		• Is there a documented system in place?		• Is the leader providing consistent, repetitive training?		Does the RG/Organization have a meaningful, written vision?
What will others feel?		• Is the documented system up to date and based on best practices?		• Is the leader training using DPO? (Demonstrate, Practice, Observe)		Does the vision connect to the result? (If so, how?)
Why does the result matter to the RG(s)?		• Do(es) the RG(s) have the necessary tools?		• Does the leader consistently follow up with the RG(s)?		Does the RG/Organization have a clearly defined, selfless cause?
When do you need to achieve this result?		• Are the tools up to date and of the best quality?		• Is(are) the RG(s) consistently reporting to the leader?		Does the cause connect to the result? (If so, how?)

Which one next step will you focus on? (Be sure to gather and process according to *Time Management Fundamentals*.")

DAVECRENSHAW

For a full-sized download of this worksheet, visit: **DaveCrenshaw.com/resulthour**

SYSTEM TEMPLATE

On the next page is a template I use in my
leadership coaching with C-level executives,
entrepreneurs, and managers. It will help
you create a single-page system for members
of your organization.

Again, you are welcome to print this out and
reuse it for your personal use, but please do
not reprint this or adapt it for professional
use without written permission.

PART 1

Define the result of the system on the left-
hand side. Answer each "result-based" question. This is critical to get everyone on the
same page. It's been said that we tell a person
we respect why something should be done,
but we tell a person we do not respect simply
what to do. You want to show the members
of your organization respect by offering a
clear understanding as to *why* this system is
so important.

PART 2

Decide who you or your team will be accountable to. This is not the person who is the Result-Getter. Rather, it is a manager or executive who will be following up with people, making sure that they're getting the result. Typically, it's best to list position title here rather than names, to keep the system timeless.

PART 3

Determine who the Result-Getters are. These are the people who will do the hands-on work to follow the system to completion. Again, I recommend using position titles rather than names.

PART 4

Dictate which traits and skills are required to master this system. Remember, traits are inherent to a person's nature. They are human characteristics or physical abilities. Skills are abilities learned over time. If the RGs trying to execute this system lack required traits, they are likely to fail. However, if they lack skills, accountability leaders can take time to teach those skills to them.

PART 5

Define the tools that will be used to follow this system. What will a person need to have to get their result? It could be as simple as an Android phone, or as complicated as productivity software. Whatever may be needed to build this system, put it in that square.

PART 6

Determine the "how" part of your system. This begins with your "trigger event." This is the event that sets the wheels of your system in motion. Once that is defined, write out all the steps one will need to get this result. Remember, your steps don't have to be perfect. There's no such thing as a perfect system, only the next draft.

PART 7

Practice using this system. As you do, you'll uncover areas for improvement. When you find those improvements, revise the system and update it with new best practices.

THE RESULT SYSTEM TEMPLATE

THE RESULT	HOW
What does a successful result look like?	Trigger Event:
What are the numbers?	
What will you feel?	
What will others feel?	
Why does the result matter to the RG(s)?	
When do you need to achieve this result?	

Who is providing **Accountability**?
Who is/are the RG(s)?
Role(s)

Traits Required	Skills Required

With what **tools**?

For a full-sized download of this worksheet, visit: **DaveCrenshaw.com/resulthour**

WORKING WITH DAVE CRENSHAW

ONLINE LEARNING

Dave's collection of online training, including the time management courses mentioned in this book, are available through LinkedIn Learning. Visit **DaveCrenshaw.com/Learn** to see his full library.

SPEAKING

Dave is available for live keynote speeches, seminars, webinars, and workshops around the world. You can request more information at **DaveCrenshaw.com/Speak**.

Made in the USA
Monee, IL
10 July 2021